kitchen sink poetry

something for everyone

elliot m rubin

ISBN
paperback # 979-8-9922464-7-6
EPub   # 979-8-9922464-8-3

Library of Congress Control Number
#2025904352

Published 2025
Elliot M Rubin
Monroe Township
N.J.

Dedication

To my grandchildren Shane,
Isabelle, Jonathan, Carter,
Alexandra, Melanie, Mollie, and Madison

In memory of my father

Herman S. Rubin
who wrote poetry, prayers and letters all his life

Preface

I believe poetry is to be read and understood by
all, and it needs to be written, for the most part, in
plain language for everyone's enjoyment.

Too often, poets write in-depth, penetrating poems
where you need to be well-read and/or versed in
literary minutia to appreciate the poetry, not this book
or any of my writings. I try to write so everyone can
enjoy a few moments of intellectual satisfaction
without consulting a dictionary or encyclopedia all
the time.

Disclaimer

This book of poetry is not intended to be read
by prudes, political book-banning conservatives,
and/or sexually inhibited and repressed small-
minded dolts.

Table of Contents

ESCAPE 8

DEITY 9

HAPPINESS 10

DEPRESSING POETRY AT 4 AM 11

PUSHING EIGHTY 12

TEXAS 13

BREAKFAST IN BROOKLYN 14

FRUSTRATION 15

WAITING AT EVERY BABY'S BIRTH 16

CEMETERY VISITS ARE SO FORLORN 17

WHERE IS HOME 18

TRAVELS 19

WHAT'S FAME 20

ALABAMA 21

YOLANDA 22

MYTHOLOGY OF PANTHERA 23

CALENDAR 24

DECISION 25

THE ALPHABET 26

IN FLEMING'S STYLE 27

SEASONAL CHANGE 28

POWER OF A HAT 29

WEEDS 30

WOKE UP 31

CONGRESS 32

SNIPPETS 33

MET HER PARENTS FOR THE FIRST TIME 34

ENGAGEMENT 35

INSURRECTION 36

REVISITING CHILDHOOD 37

SELF-JOURNEY 38

ASHES IN MY HAND 39

SONNET MAN [ODE TO BILL] 40

WHAT DOES IT MATTER WHO SOMEONE MARRIES? 41

FIRST LOVE 42

RAINBOW SUITES HOTEL 43

PERSONAL 44

WIND 45

KAVORKIAN 46

YOU PEOPLE 47

TEARS AND DEATH.. 49

KINDER KINDLING 50

UNNAMED LOVER 51

POETIC EDITING 52

NATURE'S WAY... 53

MY POETIC ROAD 54

LOST AT SEA 55

WHEN THE DINER RAN OUT OF FOOD 56

OLD FLAMES 57

TAYLOR SWIFT 58

CAMPING... 59

FUNERAL WEATHER....................................... 60

SHADOWS 61

SCHOOL GAMES 62

REFLECTIONS ON LIFE 63

I LOVE YOU 64

FATHER'S DAY 2023 65

SIDEWALKS 66

THEY SING IN CHURCH................................. 67

TOO MUCH COMPANY 68

EVIL EMPIRE 69

SHELLY 16... 70

FEET 71

SIT BY ME 72

GERRYMANDER PARTY 73

REGRETS 74

AMOROUS 75

OCEAN CITY N.J. AMUSEMENTS 2023 76

VACATION IN OCEAN CITY N.J. 2023 77

I WHISPER SOFTLY 78

EMPTINESS... 79

HURRICANE 80

MY COUNTRY 'TIS OF THEE 81

EVERYDAY A BLESSING................................. 82

DOCTOR DOCTOR[1] 83

LAWNS... 84

PATIENCE 85

UNNAMED WOMAN.. 86

CAR RIDE 87

TO CREATE 88

LOOKING AHEAD 89

JUST DESSERTS 90

AMERICAN LUDDITES 91

REMARRIAGE AGAIN 92

ANGST 93

WEEDING A GARDEN 94

WAITING 95

LIFE-LONG FRIENDS 96

CONFLICT RESOLUTION 97

IT'S OUR FIRST DATE 98

NEVER 99

1A 100

TIME 101

CROTCH DANCING 102

TO MY FIRST DAUGHTER 103

FIRE AND FLAMES 104

FLOWERS OF UKRAINE 105

EVEN THE BBC 106

SKIN AND BONES 107

LOCK UP 108

TEXAS PAN-HANDLE 109

NOT IN MY AMERICA 110

ODE TO RICHARD COREY 111

ORCHESTRA 112

MENTAL STABILITY 113

TRUTH 114

escape

five-year-old madison
a hurricane in pajamas
whizzes
through breakfast cereal,
as a waterfall of milk
cascades down
a mountain of multicolor
sugar squares to splash puddles
on a pink plastic tablecloth
similar to the backyard's lakes
where she cakes her clothes
on mother nature's muddy ground
chases butterflies,
then jumps,
shouts **wait**, and
fills the air with giggles and laughs
as the former caterpillar
struggles
to lift itself to safety   and
evade a death sentence
in a sealed glass bottle
brought into kindergarten
for a science day of show and tell

deity

flowers of death are picked
from the garden of life, before
the good farmer was ready to leave–
his flock shocked
at his departure
love and sadness fill the air
with a belief
their fields will flower forever
in his memory
if they believed in his goodness–
satan laughed and
lilith made cocktails
to celebrate another soul plucked
from earth's chaos and toils
to leave bewilderment
on earth below

happiness

we can be happy
if we're reciprocated
first, we need to give

depressing poetry at 4 am

life is a giant child's slide
you start at the bottom
struggle to climb a ladder
achieve success, then
slide down and enjoy the ride —
at the end, at the bottom,
when you die,
friends, relatives
disassemble the slide
you spent years building, and
sell the parts for scrap,
pennies on the dollar
leave nothing behind
to show you ever existed,
except memories

i must stop writing at 4 am
a raging thunderstorm outside
tap dances on my windows
in harmony with my post-surgery
pulsating mouth–
depressive words sputter from my fingers
i think of the blind/deaf poet
who feels tree bark, tenderness of a leaf, and
is published in a literary magazine
i've tried for years of submissions to be in,
and now i am able to put together
a book of rejections

pushing eighty

the old backyard wheelbarrow's rusty
you push it and hear squeaks and rattles
its only wheel wobbles
its useful life almost gone

it can't be used anymore
the match stick-legs ache
with pain in the aged joints and
like my hair, paint peels off the top

energetic sports cars whiz pass
red, yellow, and bright blue
with an engine's mighty throaty roar
reminds me of my youth, long gone

conversation is now an active sport
decisions flow like molasses
arthritic fingers tap to beats
occasionally   when i can hear the music

miss friends and family
almost all have long since gone
only my old children and grandkids are left
to wake me on visits with a soft kiss

texas

she lay moaning
at the bottom
of an ocean
of tears and heartbreak

a flaccid body, still,
while burnt-out emotions
seep slowly out
to leave an empty shell

legal sharks circle
wait to feed in court
on a broken heart
because in utero died, and
mentally destroyed a nurturer

denied a doctor's procedure
health and science secondary
to religious zealots' zeal
and women's medical rights
eventually lead to two deaths

breakfast in brooklyn

shades are up
sun yellows the room
outlines a sheer nightgown
            he sits to her right

last night was not enough —
as she lifts the milk bottle
to pour it into her hot coffee
he mentally undresses her

liquor muddles his mind
almost sober
tries to remember her name
they only met last night

they don't speak
no need
they each took what they desired
today is the next day

after re-introductions
smiles, kisses, almost say goodbye
they decide to revisit last night
one more time, m

frustration

nebulous editors decide
      we never meet them
      or even speak to them
yet we write to them
with our hearts and minds in words,
pages and filled books
which we hope they read,
understand, and want to publish–
yet too often, the thank you letter
arrives with words of encouragement
and disappointment
because what we wrote
did not strike their fancy   today,
tomorrow   maybe
with a cup of coffee
or night of lust
they wake up feeling better, and
take a liking to an early morning read–
maybe mine?

waiting at every baby's birth

the long, cold fingers
of the angel of death
grasps steel forceps
to assist in welcoming
an eventual soul
into the world
to either prosper or not,
it doesn't matter —
all babies end up dead
the question is when;
is it in youth, adulthood, or
as an elderly person; and
what have they done in life —
did they barely survive
or did they achieve,
in truth, does it matter —
tomorrow will come
yesterday will be gone
today is fleeting
everything is a memory
soon forgotten

cemetery visits are so forlorn

always a wind whirling whispers
in my mind
i dread going to see my parents
to tell them my goings and comings
they never comment on them
while i wait for answers
it seems like forever
as i try to remember
their voices of encouragement and caring,
while the short memorial plants
with small yellow and white weed flowers
spring up through the thickets
shiver with breezes along with my body,
especially in winter, when arctic winds
blow in to freeze my tears
and rend my heartbreak even more
with the realization i'm now an adult orphan
in an adult world, with other adults   who seem
well-adjusted without guidance from family,
yet i grieve and miss them

where is home

a snail is a slow mover
no dashes or darts
left or right,
steady, straight-ahead
home carried on its back
as it travels along   alone

although my home
is not on my back
it is still with me
    as i go
your love is in my soul
wherever i travel
our home is my rock
your being my fortitude
i carry it everywhere

travels

the holstein bull is satisfied
in a pasture filled with cows,
tall green grass to munch,
freedom to walk wherever,
only fences on the farm's edges
restrain him to a certain area,
there is no reason
to swim the shallow creek to escape

i can't swim to europe
hike the alps,
eat swiss cheese,
visit brothels of amsterdam,
trek the apian trail,
sleep in hostels in germany,
drive along the amalfi coast,
or fly there either, because
i too am satisfied with life as it is

what's fame

some people
climb mountains
others are athletes
a handful write best-selling novels
or a scientist finds a new drug

surprisingly
as a poet, it's not being published
in *the new yorker magazine–*
but there's one claim
which surely acknowledges fame,
a *new york times* crossword puzzle
which has eleven boxes across
to fill in my full name

alabama

white
   black
voting rights
   voting slights
supremacy
   inferiority
freedom
   serfdom
exalted
   subjugated
peaceful
   revolution
quiet
   riot
traditional values
   contemporary values
resist change
   complacency resistance
change?
   maybe eventually!

yolanda

her young supple skin,
blemish free,
glistens with beads of anticipation–
desires enter fulfillment
to rest on white billows
of soft satin sheets
in the darkness of evening–
the first time, their
skin gently presses together
fingers entwined

like the wind,
no longer a breeze, blusters
into a tornado
twirls them
into an aftermath of reality
to realize fantasy fades quickly;
with tomorrow's sunrise
life begins anew
breakfast
and
    routine

mythology of panthera

panthera and miriam
maybe   not in love
maybe   just a fling
maybe   a rape
nobody knows
only stories exist
none verifiable

history reports
her with child
married young to another
poor and homeless
gave birth in a barn
this story might be a yarn
yet it still exists
thousands of years later

calendar

tomorrow
    yes tomorrow
i always thought in youth
    tomorrows always come
it's just another day to ex-out
    on the hanging calendar, it
hangs in mom's kitchen
hangs to remind me of school days
    then happily tear off the page
at each month's end

i made it my job

now almost eighty
    as realization hits me
there aren't many pages left
    childhood friends gone
they fail to remove their pages
    now, i do it for them

decision

waves splash
against the wooden dock
as the mysterious,
deep dark blue sea laps at me —
something primal stirs,
urges me to leave
the safety of the sands
the safety of shore
to set sail and return
to life's earliest beginning
to leave behind my land life

yet i can't leave
the chains in my life
pull stronger than the sudden urges
of desire's pressure to act;
maturity immobilizes me as
her illness and impending death
weigh heavy on my decision to stay

the alphabet

contains all my friends
their foibles and successes

with each letter
          a slash of intent
each vowel
      the glue of words
alone
      they are meaningless

placed in a certain order
they fly with eagles
or
weigh heavy on my heart

in fleming's style

high class, stunningly beautiful
tall, thin, irresistible, in-demand muse
who wanders about life in an effortless
bounce from lover to lover; with ease
to absorb and digest their desires
while he writes novels about her at midnight
after many interludes of his (in)famous
romantic conquests spoken of years later

one evening, darkness lies next to him
then makes her move, he succumbs
to her irresistible charms, as she exerts
her will over his, and he departs quickly,
never to write again while she pens
her exploits in his style into bestsellers
of the illicit liaisons in her life
while his being submerges into her books

seasonal change

autumn rain never stops
overcast sky, dreary, drizzly
leaves turn color in death throes
as blooms of spring wilt in fall

old lady gardens are wrapped in tarps
rakes and shovels stowed away
winter storms soon arrive
with snow and ice to cover the yards

the warmth of summer is far behind
only vivid flashbacks of frolics remain
skimpy swimwear on female bodies
are now found in pictures and memories

my winter wool coat shaken out
summer clothes stored and sealed
december's blizzards drift in with fury
coffee and books will occupy my time

power of a hat

a blue, new york football giants hat
makes me visible when worn
strangers stop and talk to me
how do you think they'll do this year

i don't know them, or even follow the team–
years ago, the giants almost gave me ulcers!
i watched and rooted for them, but
had to stop for my health

it's not that i didn't want to watch
they could be ahead by fifty points
with only two minutes left in the game,
yet they succeeded to lose

my stomach was in a knot
right then, i decided,
i can't watch any more games
but yet, i still hope they win

now, if i don't wear the hat
i'm invisible to everybody
no one talks to me
i don't exist

weeds

she tends her garden
almost daily
plucks the invasives
when she feels a need

slyly, they crawl around
to regrow over sweet treats
and again, leaves her nothing
but stubble and short shoots

her plum tree cherished
which can be quite juicy and
a hidden red maraschino
to pluck, when found

teenage boys
are restless weeds
they never give up
to plunder her garden

woke up

ultra-right conservatives
need to woke up and realize
they have no business
in people's bedrooms; they
tell us what
consenting adults can do
in the privacy of their homes–
how does this affect them in any way?
they can't explain that whatever letters
someone affiliates with interferes
with their lifestyle?
they refuse to come forward
to demonstrate
how same-sex marriage hurts them–
not liking what you see
might bother you, but obviously
young elementary school children
blasted to smithereens
in classrooms is okay
because they only offer
thoughts and prayers to parents   and
 do nothing to prevent further murders

congress

it runs on regular order
subcommittees,
committees,
public hearings,
multiple votes,
yet it never votes
on natural order
where children should outlive parents
because too many politicians
enjoy gun lobby campaign donations, and
children die in their schools
when military weapons
splatter prepubescent bodies apart

snippets

1– he loves drink
   drink loves him
   love doesn't drink
   love seeks others
   who loves to love
   and doesn't drink
2–a homeless woman
   walks into bergdorf goodman,
   stops by a parfumerie counter
   to spray dior or chanel samples, tries
   expensive gowns in the dressing room
   to glance in a mirror; she looks and
   smells good like a fifth avenue socialite,
   but like a rose, she is still what she is
 3–it was always easy
   usually fun   when given away,
   but time took its toll
   now older, rounder, grayer,
   the quality of dates decreased,
   boyfriends now take her
   to a diner instead of for steak;
   a dim future, longed for lost youth,
   her wasted past haunts thoughts
   with the realization
   everyone gets one shot, and
   she's stuck in hers; it's now
   too late to make meaningful changes

met her parents for the first time

he went at the end of summer
start of the pre-freeze fishing season
cold outside at their mountain home
chilled down to every single bone

went inside to a nice comfy chair
sat next to the gas-burning burner
he started to warm up, and then they served
single malt whisky, shot after shot

finally stood, had to pee really bad
stands at the toilet, about to go,
felt dizzy, legs crumbled, slid down the door
ended up his ass   on the floor

afraid they heard him slide and fall
thought about what he'd tell them all
when he finally stood, he joined the fun
they were talking, oblivious to his run

engagement

mother nature doesn't rush
time runs in centuries
sometimes millenniums
things don't change
suddenly—
major shifts take eons,
like his fiancé
when asked
to marry him
her answer tarried
　　before agreeing
　　　　to be married

insurrection

hate, rage, bigotry
they seethe with the lust of turmoil
misinformed masses
follow the hollow screeded

the base fed false facts
they're better than others
book bans prevent
thinking from being taught

the golden eagle of freedom
flutters, its wings singed,
foresees the death of the republic
by those who swore allegiance

revisiting childhood

after a two-hour drive
to revisit a childhood memory
on a farm:
with a massive wood   barn,
hay strewn on the floor,
a large, well-fed cat i played
with when it was a tiny kitten,
and a pasture that held a bunch
of munching guernsey'
with a minefield of cow pies

discovered it's gone
replaced by a sprawling
low-level red brick
sterile school structure
the green fields black asphalted over
the flowing creek's swimming crook
once hidden in an oasis of trees
now off limits in the far rear
of the no-trespassing municipal property
never to visit   or swim in again

self-journey

life has twists and turns
from chasing pretty girls
to obtain an education
you never know where you'll end up

from a business degree to law school
to owning a large retail company
never did it cross my mind
i'd write crime novels at retirement

in old age, the discovery of poetry
opened a new world visioned
one of creativity and opportunity
a primal urge never felt before

ashes in my hand

with patience
waits for a big storm
with strong gusts of wind
hurricane strength

carefully, his hand reaches in
raises high overhead
as an aged palm
exposes ashes
to be blown away
hopefully
to the blue oceans she swam in,
the mountain trails she walked,
fertile fields she picnicked, and
the backs of horses she rode

last wishes
for the winds to take her
to lands she longed to visit
but illness prevented

sonnet man [ode to bill]

handcuffed
doesn't fight for freedom
masochistic tendencies
rule his writing

he rhymes on a dime
counts to ten, too
yet he can't stop because
iambic pentameter rules

enslaved to sonnets
with unbreakable chains
rarely does free verse
with words he can perse

three quatrains above
and a couplet below

what does it matter who someone marries?

tall man and a short woman
  deemed normal
tall woman and a short man
  curiosity
white man and black woman
  erotic
black man and white woman
  klan feelings
man and a man
  disgusting
woman and a woman
  sensual
inter-religious union
  troublesome
one man and two women
  polyamory accepted
two men and one woman
  polygamy unsettling
who marries who? who cares
  how does it affect you
there is no such thing
  as bad love
live with it

first love

she held him to her chest
baby lips slurped nourishment
mother's tender touches
never forgotten, always sought

baby lips sought nourishment
she held him to her chest
at twenty-five, a reflex moment
the date kissed her neck

mother's tender touches
never forgotten, always sought
baby lips sought nourishment
at twenty-five, a reflex moment

rainbow suites hotel

small solitary suites of rooms
hidden 'round the corner
cast back in shadows
between tall buildings
located downtown

tremendous terra cotta vases
flower filled overflowing
stands guard
in front of a multicolored entrance
welcome all who desire entry

immaculate detail paid attention
to every item, embroidered towels,
logos on bathrobes, carpets,
all dinnerware, plates,
also burnished on steaks'

it is a happy hotel
hot baths
hidden in the basement
greets artists, poets, politicians
able to frolic undisturbed
in a family values state

personal

how do you remember
a guiding light
they're like beautiful buildings
something sturdy
they're built to last
to be looked up at,
some think
    forever
but nothing
is made that way
sadly
this includes my mother

wind

i stand in an open field
the ground beneath
filled with family, hear
them speak to me in the wind

they whisper of sorrow and regrets
happy events missed
children and grandchildren
my tears well with tales of woe

how can i persevere   when they didn't
live longer, to enjoy progeny–
what on earth can i do
other than live as best i can
                              for them

kavorkian

death is not sought early
life's too precious,
 it's to be lived fully–
 the purpose of being
is to have generations survive,
to continue, not end,
except naturally

but disease and unbearable pain
disrupts life's plans, and with
empathy and kindness, one
rings the final bell sooner
in order to die in peace,
with dignity,
without pain

you people

are the problem
you don't understand us
we don't need to understand you
your customs and accents
are different
we don't speak like that now

our ancestors learned to adjust
you have to learn
this is america
where what was past
is now desired by many
who lack the understanding
a good education brings to civics and
what can be, is understood by those
who paid attention in school–
once we were you people, too

childhood

memories don't die
they float away till recalled
then relived again

tears and death

when will the mississippi
stop overflowing
with the tears
of heartbroken parents
whose children died
before old age
from disease and violence
because monied lobbyists
bribe politicians
to do what will benefit them,
not us, and
death can be bought freely,
without restraint,
in many gun shops
across the land
of amendment rights and
fill cemeteries to overflow
with needless burials and
mourners who will endure
unsustainable grief

kinder kindling

how many
small sticks stacked
are needed
to take flicks of flames
into the inferno of hell
where the callous live
who offer only
thoughts and prayers
instead of dousing the fires
of young gun deaths

unnamed lover

on my knees
i beg you
hold me in your arms
cradle my face to your chest
as you would a lover's bond
slide your petite hand
gently on my cheek
caress me
whisper words
my heart desires
my ears long to hear

stay

stay here

stay here with me
entangled together
forever

please

poetic editing

in isolation
my pen slides across the page
it wipes out words, lines,
stanzas remorse rears up
my day's work
destroyed it is a death

sudden

different

yet a death
like the stream's
trout it died by my
hands
a hook in its mouth
a blank stare up at
me   it wriggled in
my hands

then stopped

just as my words died
today flatness, emptiness
the life force gone

nature's way

frog legs are a delicacy
if you like tiny bites
to dig out between bones
its meat hops out at you

turtle soup is too green
you can't see the bottom
of the murky bowl
eat it very   s l o w l y

once kangaroo meat
was served at a dinner
not sure how it was prepared
but when finished.   i was jumpy

my poetic road

i dared to travel
on sacred paths of
rhythm and rhyme
which flows from their pens
fills volumes of pages
overflows on staid,
overcrowded
library shelves

immersive poems spin in my mind
some easy-to-read and understand
like robert frost's forest rhyme

it's the longer ones
which the poets demand i interpret
to read what they hide in verse
hidden treasures of dear old emily
or earthy words of bukowski, and
beat poems of ginsberg and corso–
with timidity,
i venture forth with pen and paper
on my sacred paths, of
rhythm and rhyme

lost at sea

hard to kill love
once it drops anchor
your heart pounds
with every thought
a future locked together
common sense evaporates

it leaves a salty taste when
plans planned
don't pan out, and
they abandon ship
to sail away to other ports
with the cargo of your soul

ballast's bulge of memories
grounds you on shore
prevents your sails from
billowing once more
only to wish their ship return
to your dock forever

when the diner ran out of food

early morning
or at dusk
a red fox can be seen
it slithers and scurries
between homes, bushes, and trees
in search of food

lately
it hasn't been noticed slinking about
    gone
     maybe
because squirrels disappeared, too
once   they were everywhere
up trees, down trees, they'd
scamper about everywhere
now none
nowhere here
nowhere there
they're gone,
with the missing fox

old flames

sometimes i forget
something of value, but i
do remember you

taylor swift

i wanna be a swifty
dress outrageously,
blend in with thousands
flow with her tunes
sing along
mouth every word
belt out every melody
    with my idol
to remember her set
i wanna be a groupie
at each concert
it's an adult's teen desire
even though i did retire
to feel young again
i wanna be a swifty

camping

darn, bugs everywhere
they climb on trees
crickets clamor all night
ants claim the ground
my sleeping bag is on;
even the leaves of trees
in the dampness of morning
spit down on me
as i lean against
a thick oak trunk
to eat my food

no
i'm not sharing food
they can have the crumbs,
the baked beans
which fell off my plate,
or the spilled sweet tea
puddled at my feet

darn, bugs everywhere i look

the best part of roughing it
is the ride back to civilization
where i can complain about
rats, feral cats, and filthy streets,
and on thursdays,
the maid vacuums

funeral weather

a bright sunny day
is not the way
to have a burial
too bright
too cheery
to say goodbye

a rainy or snowy day
makes a muddy mess
when they burrow down
to hibernate loved ones
forever shielded
from temperamental skies

but

an overcast day is perfect
no happy sun or crying skies
just dreary and drumpy
is the way to go
no muddle ground to sink in
a great day to bury away

shadows

the house creaks
from the summer storm
wind-driven rain batters windows
while sounds rebound inside

once there was a brightness
a sunshine-illuminated life
his world rotated around her
today everything is gloomy

she is gone, forever, as he
sits on the plaid, worn-out sofa,
the one they cuddled on
their fortieth anniversary

light shines on him from the table lamp
he longs for her as in the past
when they sat close together
as their shadows merged

school games

live electrical wires have
                two ends
        one positive   one negative
electric sparks flair
when opposites meet
always brings violent reactions
same as in politics
some politicians don't care
you care
killing children is the latest
non-recess school time game
played with young lives
while congress and judges
enjoy pensions and perks
and parents tend cemetery plots

reflections on life

life's like a broadway play
    done in three acts
first act
    youth start strong
second act
    middle age builds foundations
third act
    retirement, the encore
finally
    the curtain lowers
hopefully
    the audience applauds
says good things
    about the actor in their reviews
though never gets to hear them

i love you

she wrote to me
i thought
    thank you   love you too
but did not write her back
though we will never touch,
share food on a plate,
or sleep softly ensconced in bed
romantically embraced

the distance of miles and
other long-term commitments
is too great a chasm to leap

we will write while we can
of a special bond
which stirs in our loins
longing to connect
until someday,
a day i believe,
will probably never come

father's day 2023

i don't remember his voice
though i heard it
for   forty   years
memory   fades
three decades since

his warmth
his humor
his humanity helping hearts
in need of an outstretched hand
recalled he
always offered assurance, assistance

sat at his desk writing
poems
prayers
prose

i think of my father today
with his large heart
the one that eventually failed him

sidewalks

her pale color
fades even more
under an overcast yellow sun
eyes blink
impossible
to look for long
thin, underfed, waifs
left in the streets to pity
    society's throwaways
unable to care for themselves
    invisible bodies
not noticed enough in one's life
    the wealthy are blind to them
    as they enter private entries
    doorman guarded
ignorant of the fact
the economy made many,
like themselves,
into concrete huggers and outcasts
ignored by politicians and others
unless inconvenienced

they sing in church

praise the lord
everything's his doing

  -the death of mothers from sepsis due
to politicians preventing abortions of a
dead fetus
  - the shooting deaths
of hundreds of innocent children in
school classrooms
  - illnesses and injuries
medically not treated
because health care not offered -
  addicted mothers
birthing addicted children

the fallen angel
rejoices
as he devours
politicians' souls
while people praise in
church

too much company

waves of the atlantic
roll over burning beaches at coney island
an overabundance of sunbathers
shoulder to shoulder
run into the surf
splashing and laughing
with sun umbrellas staked deep
its arms outstretched
to cover a flannel blanket table
with a picnic basket of food at the ready–
i bought a summer house up north
buried in a valley gulch
surrounded by deeply treed virgin mountains
where winds funnel over
cold, fast water creeks
to cool summer heat–
alone in silence
serenity covers me
until relatives arrive
they left the city behind
to frolic and sprinkle their joy
loudly
in bucolic forests
to rattle trees and bushes
with a city's gyrating noise
think everyone deserted the beach

evil empire

there are so many to choose from
a dictator can be labeled a president
human rights jailed, killed, denied, and
accepted as normal by everyone
except those crawling
under the yoke of oppression
until eventually, in life,
everything will end in death
floods recede
volcanoes go dormant
life goes on   elsewhere

shelly 16

she was a heartbreaker
but it was my heart;
hurt then   but
years flow on
a rushing river of time
dulls teenage pain,
though still remembered

my first kiss,
long hugs,
a summer romance,
a movie made,
novels, and
an old poet's free verse poem
of lost love
written about

feet

published by Chewers & Masticadores September 2023

1

toes are pretty far from a nose
yet fresh from a hot sweaty sneaker
wash them with a garden hose
everyone knows toes perspire

2

in the back is a sturdy ankle
holds the body's total weight
it's the last thing to shoehorn in
no matter if the body is thick or thin

3

paint those nails a pretty pink
to match a gown shiny and slink
doesn't matter if a foot is wide
a pretty shoe is needed to hide

4

pick the grapes off a vine
fill the tub for a smash
with bare feet, make a dash
from all sides, stomp the mash

5

feet, feet, pretty ugly
they might stink
yet
   still neat

sit by me

published by Juste Literacy May 2024

the old wooden pier
is peaceful
my legs hang
as cool mountain lake water
flows through toes
small sunfish scoot under
while listless, i watch
a lone hawk spread magnificent
circles the water
small birds hide in trees
which line the shoreline
like a waistband holding back a bloated dinner

the sun has passed noon
shadows float out from the shoreline
reaching, stretching, trying
to cover everything it can, and
eventually will
but i should be gone by then
building a fire encased by ancient stones
dug out when my home's foundation was formed,
and the underbrush
pruned back, trees cleared, land leveled
allows me to relax and
view humanity's vision of nature
when back on my old wooden dock

gerrymander party

a political party says
it wants to protect people
they mouth meaningless words
about self-liberties and rights
yet their politicians control voting rights
take away constitutional rights
say they will protect those rights
in reality, ignore these rights

let's realize the raw hypocrisy
before we vote in the fall

regrets

i regret to inform you
i have regrets in my life
from simple things like
not sincerely asking
how do you feel today
to a close friend,
or about the date i ghosted
decades ago, in my youth,
because i didn't want to go
to a halloween costume party
on the train, now haunts me

age brings clarity
to memories;
with stickpins to my heart
maturity chastens me
to make amends
knowing it's impossible
and the self-flagellation
continues unabated

amorous

beautiful roses
like in the all-night diner
    takes time to grow strong
might be a thorn
    to overcome
yet in bloom
    lovely to behold

it lives
    then eventually dies,
when the life force
    stem is cut, and
the flower slowly fades,
    its tender petals fall away

yet the fragrance
    continues to live
forever
    in memories

ocean city n.j. amusements 2023

i sit on a wooden bench
under a roller coaster
while a thunderous roar
shatters stillness
my young granddaughters
scream in fright as they ride in
cars that shimmy and shake
race up and down
twist and turn
until gravity exhausts the ride

a marching band
struts past me on the boardwalk
with a heavy-set drum major
who wildly waves a long gold baton
while he high-steps about
in a tight fit
glitter-tasseled-gold costume
both my little girls stand motionless,
watch a short parade pass
then run into
an overstuffed candy store
to feast on plastic bags
of sweet, multi-colored, gummy fish

vacation in ocean city n.j. 2023

pack this and that
don't forget
those things on the counter,
you know,
the ones we never use
but might–
throw them in the bag over there,
not the first one
but the ninth, the red one,
then pack the car–
i hope we can leave before lunch

finally loaded, the back seat overflows,
trunk filled, slowly the lid closes
a gentle push seals everything in
not even a skinny,
undernourished church mouse
could finagle itself in there.

then the realization
we have to do it again in one week
probably with souvenirs, too–
wonder
if i left a kid behind
would anyone be missed

i whisper softly

as we walk through life together
place your hand in mine
i'll stay by your side forever
don't ever let go

i searched for many years
you are my soulmate
our future entwined by love
our past alone has passed

i'll sit by your side all night
pray you survive this wicked illness
memories of us torrentially gush back
i fear tomorrow will come too soon

emptiness

he stands on the corner
watches everything
expressionless
motionless
stares straight ahead
as people pass   and
ignore him

now a blank mind
     once famous
a human treasure of words
his books of poems sold out
edition after published edition
 stacked and stored in libraries

a dutiful daughter comes along
slowly,
      they walk home
he tends to wander away
sometimes, it's all-day
before she finds him–
thank god for my sister

hurricane

hastily
it sweeps along
over the ocean's warm waves
it's eye calm, yet it
builds **strength**
rain steady
then torrential
winds *pick up speed*
they spiral,
burl, and twirl
cars and trees about
then leaves
devastation
death and
destruction behind

a memorial storm
remembered forever
like my daughter's divorce

my country 'tis of thee

america
once was aspirational
it preached fairness
equality for all
although never wholly followed
enough was done
to be seen as truth–
now, *there are good people
on both sides*
white nationalists, fascists, and
authoritarian followers
are told to
stand by and be ready
by our leader, as
fringe populations, minorities,
are considered less–
what happened
to the american way,
everyone's guaranteed
a good education
a rounded background
aware of facts, not hidden–
years of closeted darkness opened
where light can shine in
has disappeared
the door slammed shut, and
federal courts hold the key
to unlock it–
in time, democracy will
either flourish or dehydrate
in a slow   agonizing death spiral
i pray no

everyday a blessing

as dusk darts in, and the
sun falls behind the horizon, darkness
rises to settle down over everything

a young redheaded girl swirls tufts
of hair wrapped around a finger, and
looks out her bedroom window

she sees firefly fairies dance in the field
once the playground of young pirates, who
swash-buckled on imaginary adventures

only her mind is free to run about barefoot
the tubes and wires of life restrict her body;
outside is thought of every day inside

it's not fair   her distraught parents rant, yet
her calmness in the face of death unsettles them—
she is self-assured the fairies will soon play with her

doctor doctor[1]

the late news channel announced tonight
their medical doctor, who gave advice
to keep us healthy and active in life
died

when the know-it-all doctor dies
what hope is there
we don't know what he knew
who is going to advise us medically

when the family doctor is booked up
only a walk-in clinic is open
the doctor there may not be back
who will follow up if needed

a television physician is a necessity
the doctor always looks us in the eye, and
speaks to us, clearly and plainly, they give
us guidance when chaos overcomes our lives

what hope is there
when the doctor dies

---

[1] September 2023 when Dr. Max Gomez of CBS-TV died

lawns

the green grass of summer
grows every year
needs water and mowing
always a chore
like the sun rises in the east

life is the lawn
in everyone's town
it grows
needs shaping and shearing
until autumn arrives
then turns brown
withers
        dormant

when spring arrives
rain waters it
then again it thrives

sometimes disease kills
and a gardener buries it in mulch
reseeds, and a new life is born
as the homeowner remembers
how beautiful the lawn used to look
waiting to shape, shear, cut

patience

at 3:30 am not much to do
except read
an early news aggregator
on my computer   it kills time
before my oral surgery in five hours,
then watch the dawn yawn
to chase away night darkness
as the sun rises bright
while i decide teeth don't last
no matter how many times
you brush, floss, or visit a dentist
extractions are like medical divorces
a painful parting
costs a lot of money, and
not much to show afterward
except for an empty wallet and mouth

she was hesitant
embarrassed
    to show them
not born this way
because of diseased genetics
they are not normal
they look abnormal
        after removal
surgery tried to replace them

afterward
sunlight never shines there
until she met someone special
who lifted her shirt and
loved her for her
not society's image of womanhood
        she deserves happiness
everyone deserves happiness

car ride

three of them in the car
crowded, elbow to elbow,
the road's bumpy
with sharp, unyielding curves
as the three brothers,
all sons of abraham
fight amongst themselves
trying to push each other
out of a moving car.
two in the front, big guys,
while the third son in the rear seat
is very small,
but stands his ground and
can't be bullied—
bystanders wait and watch
who will eventually walkout
when the car finally stops

to create

traffic flows fast
stoplights slow it to a crawl
creativity is similar
except it sputters and
doesn't move smoothly
sometimes it stops
you can turn the key often
the motor will start
when it catches a spark

sometimes, once it does
it doesn't stop
morning
afternoon
night time
3 am

exhausted

when the gears
finally crank, creak, spurt
they turn out stanzas ad nauseum
until exhaustion sets in, and
the engine needs to add oil
with a good night's sleep

looking ahead

my life floats down
the mighty mississippi of life past
the beached raft unrestrained
huckleberry used whom i was
jealous of in youth and the white
picket fences
of st.petersburg missouri
where my childhood mind e x p a n d e d to
see my friends
who left before me as
        they wave to me
from the sloppy mud banks
as the dirt dikes further downstream,
break, to allow memories of family to
flood consciousness and
bring them back to life in my mind's eye–
not far ahead
i see new orleans and the
mouth of the river where
it empties out
and my trip of decades will end

just desserts

lucifer is busy cleaning house,
commands the tortured souls of purgatory
to make space for new arrivals

his handiwork on earth is fulfilling
wars, famine, inhumane suffering
despicable minions listen to his orders

with much glee, the angel of death,
with gusto does his job
sends the maladjusted to flames

upset innocents rise to heaven
pain extinguished, forgotten, sutured,
never to return, to luxuriate amongst clouds

he looks for more maladjusted souls

american luddites

woe is this country
as societal luddites lurk
everywhere–
they've banned books,
raised the banner of woke,
invaded womb decisions and
intend to build a society
based on big business's
political donations, while
sugarcoated lies
tell the uninformed and undereducated
their medical resources are being denied
to protect and prevent
a socialist society
taking away their rights
as they die of curable disease
and violent gun deaths
in schools and public places

remarriage again

processional music starts,
chapel's rear doors open,
slowly, the wedding party
walks down the aisle
the groom stops at the front
to watch groomsmen and bridesmaids
hand in hand, approach,
suddenly, he notices
his secret is in the wedding party;
he did not expect to see her today—
his second marriage
the bride's third,
they decided to spend their life together
they met only a few months before
at a nudist pizza party
became aware they had a lot in common—
they both wanted an open marriage
after previous unions ended due to infidelity;
this one, though, will have no secrets or inhibitions,
they thought–
the officiant smiles at the bride
as he starts the service,
only she knows   he, is her secret

angst

as a senior citizen, a person
has collected many life experiences
occasionally some pop up
in one's consciousness

as i think back to years ago
i wonder if the threats teachers made
truly ended up on my permanent record
or did the words slink away in invisible ink

oh, so many nights of prayer for
the school principal to lose them
or the building should catch on fire
nobody would rush in to save them

i feared my parents would see them
not that i did a lot of naughty things
but you know, we all did something,
hopefully, mine didn't end up
                    in the smithsonian

weeding a garden

the young bird grew,
walked to the edge, then
jumps from its nest
as her wings spread out,
glides with the wind and
looks for safe landing

everything's different
when not in the safety net
of a parent's home, the young
chick seeks a nest of her own

as a young adult, she's
beautiful and desired
by the males
who constantly flock to her,
too many to handle;
doesn't want to fly around
with too many males as
she's not that type
it forces her to garden and
weed out the ones
not suitable to nest with

waiting

time feels like forever

until death visits

enjoy the colorful blooms of life

while they blossom in your spring

life-long friends

we were planted about the same time
strong, as young trees are supposed to be
to grow tall with sturdy roots and branches
as years passed, we grew thick together

now mature, i notice a few trees no longer here
parasites or disease caused their demise
their leaves no longer appear on branches
slowly, they disappeared, chopped down in youth

now aged, the senior trees fall fast
my friends are fewer and fewer; they are missed
i realize my roots aren't as strong anymore
branches now sag from storms; days left numbered

conflict resolution

early morning sun
peeks over the horizon
armed men burst in
death surges
father killed   while asleep
two children try to hide
not successful
young mother scooped up
flung over a shoulder
spirited away
to be sold as a slave
held hostage
given as a concubine
then passed around
an object with no humanity

this is history, past and present
for millennia, nothing changes

it's our first date

she's next to me
i'm nervous
her hand reaches out
soft skin slides over mine
fingers find fingers to interlock
i'm nervous
start to perspire
my arm reaches around her
gently i pull her closer
before the fun starts
this is my first time i told her
    don't worry, it's not mine,
    i've done this many times already
i'm nervous   and perspire even more
she leans closer
my senses tingle with anticipation
our heads so close
suddenly without warning
the roller coaster starts to rumble
the wild ride begins
up and down
curves never experienced before
up and down
finally
        exhausted
                the ride
stops

never ever is a long time
when it is supposed to last
forever
          and doesn't

the most delicious fruits
eventually, decay and sour
become bitter to the tongue

to spew words from the heart
intended to wound and be mortal
never ever is a goal to attain

it will never ever   sometimes

1A

i expected a letter from my draft board
after colonel parker from the local board,
in my first year
addressed all law students one morning

third-year not yet lawyers come june
will be gone, drafted into the viet-nam war
second-year men will be allowed a third,
my first-year group will be 1a; too bad for me

luckily i had access to a fabulous law library
forget going to class, i had research to do–
what if i showed up for induction at fort-hamilton
and refused to raise my hand and step forward

drafted soon-to-be soldiers voluntarily have to
submit to military law, give up their constitutional
rights, and the answer i sought was "what if i refuse?"
could they jail me for refusing to give them up

i decided lawyers couldn't decide either,
the question remained: did i want to find out
the legal consequences in person–
that is the question, and i didn't want to be surprised

time

one day
  every day
      many days
          add up to weeks

enough days total a lifetime
it feels   slow
where did they go
can't retrieve past days
or relive them
except in memory

some people keep a diary
for each individual day
to be read by someone else
at a later date and time

or have their total days etched
in stone on grassy, forever fields
filled with tearful memorial slabs
to count the days   lived in years

crotch dancing

i see professional
rock 'n roll
dancers move to
the beat
legs shake and kick
out arms flail
their pants
tight very
tight
so tight
they need to grab
themselves as they dance
to the music

maybe if they were
looser there wouldn't
be a need to grab at
their crotch
so crotchety old
people wouldn't be so
crotchety when they
grab a crotch

to my first daughter

it's not easy to be leaned upon
siblings become your students
in old age, parents become children

youthful years spent
tutored by mom and dad
how to do the right thing

sometimes life isn't easy
expectations high
burdens heavy

you are a product of my
deep affection, molded
into a caring, love-filled woman

you are the first daughter
loved without limits
your duties fearlessly faced

believe in yourself
fly with the eagles
you are capable
you are loved

fire and flames

sirens blare
fire engines roar
traffic stops, parts
bells clang
air horns bellow
bystanders aware
danger somewhere
luckily not here

flames flare out windows
people race to the streets
hearts heave with fear
suddenly, fire-trucks stop near

hoses unpacked
bayoneted to hydrants
police arrive
families displaced
nowhere to go

heat's hotter than
jalapeño peppers with
nothing to cool it down

after, ashes are grey
belongings fizzled
burned feelings in many souls
nothing left but heartbreak colored ash

flowers of ukraine

they were a family of four
normal in every way
dad a worker; every day
mom home cleans, cooks
normal in every way

war arrives
rockets destroy their home
father never stops work
to enjoy little things in life
he volunteers

from the front lines, he sends home
pictures of trench-grown flowers
normal in every way
never seen before
beauty in life noticed
the pictures stop

war continues
normal in every way

even the bbc

principles
are meant to be kept
they are beliefs and rules
we live by, such as
only proper music can be played,
like the tea and biscuits tunes
queen elizabeth could listen to
at high tea,
not the ungodly rock 'n roll
        offshore pirate stations
                          play
for the young, uncouth of the nation
who shag to tunes–
no, there are things we don't do

until we do

long live the queen

skin and bones

everything pulsates
satiates body and soul
whenever we're one

lock up

her hair is not blonde anymore
or brunette either, only prison grey,
the former figure-eight body rounded out
to look more like a zero with long, frizzy hair
everywhere
no need to please men or herself,
those days are over; the meds took care of her needs,
so did the iron bars on her window and door
where she'll be living for another decade or more
to pay for her felony deeds–
the judge wanted to put her away forever and a day,
but on appeal, received twenty-five to life
for one huge tragic mistake– she fell in love
with a homicidal psychopath with rage swing moods
when triggered by anything, no matter how small–
in lockup, she met dozens of women
who self-defended themselves into prison
where they found safety, peace, and a new kind of love

texas pan-handle

the texas panhandle is flat scrub brush
nothing much on i40, no rush
 on the way to abilene to pick up a load
while my new red peterbilt hums along

i approach the city, a young girl in short cutoffs
on the side of the road holds a cardboard sign–
san diego scrawled in black marker, brakes
screech, eighteen-wheeler stops with a whine

she climbs in, puts a small bag behind her
how far you goin' she asks
    all the way to the ocean, where you from
the husky masculine voice answers
elko, nevada, in lana's funhouse

looks like a teenager still in high school
never would've guessed she's a working girl
thanks for the lift; want a free fun twirl
i smiled, shook my head no, and kept on driving

not in my america

there has always been bigotry
but it was always simmering
rarely boiling over
on the stove of humanity

in my city i never feared
going anywhere because of religion
today the red-hot cauldron of hate
burns out of control

openly spewed by politicians
to bar people from entering
because of religion, regardless
of the bill of rights and constitution

my country is gone, missing, stolen
right from under my nose by people
who spread innuendo and outright lies
to intimidate voters with falsehoods

their ultimate goal is power,
elections count, every vote adds up
these mongers with malice and loathing
only want to empower themselves

ode to richard corey

he spits out flowers with every word
sweet nothings
meant to soothe and smooth

a tip of the hat
a chair pulled out
society's eloquent and elegant
gentleman   they thought

deep inside
saddened and fraught
harmful musings
depressed for years

the haughty exterior
known to so many
only   a fragile facade

orchestra

the auditorium is packed
every seat filled
sides and mezzanine, too
people talk, low-level hums fill the room
the orchestra tunes their instruments
with creaks, cracks, and off-tones

tap   tap   tap

a small baton rises
the maestro waits for silence
all eyes on him

                                                        out
                                            flail
            with a quick upstroke, his arms
                                            flail
                                                        out

cellos join after a few bars
double bass fiddles rumble in
timpani drums boom in tune
beethoven is alive
his voice **strong** and *melodic*
in concert tonight
only to be a cherished memory
tomorrow

mental stability

once bold and emboldened
now, a memory
as mirrors
harshly reflect truth

people change
some grow great with age
others wither away
unable to withstand
ego shattering abuses

truth

we don't read it
we don't see it
all news is censored
"they" feel we will be upset
scenes and information
too raw
too real
because it is
we never see it
or rarely read about the atrocities
we never see it
bloody bullet-ridden bodies
of school children,
we never see it
badly beaten raped women, and
the unseemly underbelly of society
we would be outraged
things would be changed
we will never know
we don't read of it
we don't see it on television either
all news is censored

the end

Thank you for reading my poetry

For other books of poetry written by
me please visit my personal website:

<u>www.CreativeFiction.net</u>

To follow me on Instagram, go to:

elliot_m_rubin

people poems

www.ingramcontent.com/pod-product-compliance
Lightning Source LLC
Chambersburg PA
CBHW071537100726
47908CB00004B/1412